DREAMS
FROM
A
WINTRY
NIGHT

To Allan and Karen

with affectionate regards and
best wishes for a happy and
fruitful (literarily and otherwise)
New Year.

Niles

Old Lyme
XII. 92

Also by Niles Bond:

Poetry

Arcanum (1965)

Elegos (1967)

DREAMS FROM A WINTRY NIGHT

*

POEMS

BY

NILES BOND

Foreword by CHARLTON OGBURN

THE BROOKDALE PRESS

Stamford, Connecticut

For information, address the publisher:
THE BROOKDALE PRESS
184 Brookdale Road,
Stamford, Connecticut 06903

International Standard Book Number: 0-912650-07-9
Library of Congress Catalog Number: 92-74261

FIRST PRINTING

Manufactured in the United States of America by
RAY FREIMAN & COMPANY, Stamford, Connecticut 06903

To
the Memory
of
Beloved Julia

Contents

Foreword

Seldom have I read poetry with which I have found myself so intimately identified, that expresses so eloquently what I have felt, and which has moved me so much. I marvel at the lucidity and simplicity with which this poet reveals the complicated pain of existence. His cogency, clarity, and genuineness give to his poems a power and direction I rarely find in the published poetry I read.

In this world of organized emotions and distracting cacophony, how gratefully one turns to such a record of feeling in solitude.

CHARLTON OGBURN

(Author of *The Marauders,*
The Gold of the River Sea,
The Winter Beach,
*The Mysterious William
Shakespeare: the Myth and
the Reality,* and other books.)

DREAMS
FROM
A
WINTRY
NIGHT

DARKHARBOR

That dawn will come
When I shall go down
Unclothed
Across this gull-swept shingle
To the sea;
And as one descends
The long hill into town,
So shall I walk down the shore's slow fall,
Past breaking surf,
Until the sea becomes my sky
And the fish my birds;
And I shall go on,
Down the eastward-dropping plains,
Until I hear the sea-logged tolling
Of bells
From the dead ships,
Scattered like ruined churches
Across the sea's dark country;
And the wary eyes of sea beasts,
Grazing the kelp-brown slopes,
Will follow me
Into the deepening gloom;
And I shall arrive at last
Where no light dares to go,
And in the mute darkness of that place
Will be my journey's end.

IMPERIAL PALACE, KYOTO

The ghosts who walk these halls by night
Are not alone.
Beneath the teeming silence
Of these sleeping rooms
They hear the furtive sound
Of foxes,
Burrowing through the underpinnings
Of a dynasty.

Wild foxes,
Old beyond the memory of man,
Irreverent creatures of the night,
Unmoved by the swaying panoply
Of majesty
Which through uncounted seasons
Did saturate these precincts
With the incense of divinity,
The smell of blood,
The pungent odor of a passion
Locked like a soundless scream
Behind the brittle armor-plate
Of ritual.

They care not,
These brush-tailed saboteurs,
For history.
Nor do they fear
The sudden cataclysmic end,
When massive beams of cypress

Will shudder one last time
And fall,
Bringing down the edifice of ages
Upon their backs.

They care not, fear not,
But go on burrowing
Through the roots of time,
Knowing naught
But that the dawn will come
And they will sleep.

FOR GIOVANNA IN AUTUMN

Never will you lie with me
In the burnished dawn
On some Tyrrhenian beach,
Shedding the velvet chrysalis
Of sleep
To welcome love's delight.

And never shall I lie with you
In the dappled shade
Of lemon groves,
Drunk with the bread and wine
Of our communion.

Never shall we lie together;
For this is Autumn
And I am Autumn's child
As you are Spring's;
And as the great slow wheel
Of seasons
Turns
And buoyant Spring ascends
Toward Summer's warmth,
Doomed Autumn falls inexorably
Toward Winter's death.

We shall not lie together;
But we will love
With the tough sinew
Of our minds,

Forging dark secrets
From the chaste hunger
Of our hearts,
Till that day comes
When we shall part
Forever,
When you will turn away
Toward Summer's destiny
While I,
In the gray too-lateness of my time,
Remain behind,
Loving you in the quiet grieving way
That old men have
Of dreaming dreams,
While listening for the far call
Of the curlew
At the edge of night.

SOLILOQUY AFTER HANGING UP ONE'S CLOAK AND DAGGER FOR THE FINAL TIME

My war is done;
And yet,
In this air-conditioned vacuum,
I live still on the verge
Of great and terrible acts:
Plotting revolutions
Of the mind,
Contriving Armageddons
Of the soul,
Listening for half-remembered passwords
In the night,
Searching abandoned walls
For cabalistic hieroglyphs
Whose portents
I alone can read.

I live still on the verge
Of great and terrible acts,
And on this verge,
Before the unplumbed depths
Of doom,
I build my Bethlehem,
Well-shored against the fall.

HOW DOES ONE LEARN?

How does one learn
To live again
When one has been for too long
Dead?

How does one learn
To speak again
When one has been for too long
Mute?

How does one learn
To sing again
When one has been for too long
Deaf?

How does one learn again
The words of love
When one has been too long
Alone?

> If I could but reach out
> To know your touch,
> To feel the pulse-beat of your soul,
> To be drawn once more
> Into the haven of your body,
> Then would I live and speak and sing
> Again;
> Then would I know again
> The long-forgotten words of love.

CALIFORNIA RED

Ruby,
Burning
In the shadow's fork,
Turning the Sun's pure light
To blood.

Red Ibis
On a field of snow,
Hackles shimmering
With each tremor
Of our slightest move.

Arrow,
Paling red,
Falling upward
Toward its rendezvous
With emptiness.

TO STRIVE TOWARD LIGHT

Is this our Fate...

To strive toward Light,
Out from that inner core
Of darkness,
Out of the seed,
Out of the egg,
Out of the primal womb;

To strive toward Light,
To struggle outward
Through the dark concentric prisons
Of the Being
Toward the outer ring;

To strive toward Light,
To struggle upward
From the buried cities of the Mind,
Up through the silted ages
Toward the sun;

To strive toward Light,
To flee the dark,
To struggle outward, upward,
And then break free at last —
Into a darker darkness;

To strive toward Light,
And only darkness find?

REPLY TO RALA

"and I acknowledge but one God —
man's own free mind,
that small, coiled, poisonous scorpion
with its threatening tail."

KAZANTZAKIS, *The Odyssey*

This
You would make your God?

This puny arthropod,
Scuttling across the vast indifferent slopes
Of that insomnious volcano
Which is the Heart,
Fleeing in terror
At every tremor
From the Heart's deep molten core
Of pain and ecstasy?

This is the terrible scorpion of the mind
Which you would make your God?

Then beware!
For when that volcano which is the Heart
Erupts,
A thousand scorpions die.

MUSICA VITAE

A leaden bell
Tolling
In the strangled chamber of the gut;
The moan of wind
Whimpering
Through the splintered rafters
Of the brain;
An idiot song from a moss-grown tongue,
Crooned in the bat-shrill dusk
Before the soul's long night.

No crystal shards of music now,
No whispered hymns of love,
No lark-bright dawns;
No longer these,
But a soundless dirge
Played on an unstrung clavier
In a darkening room.

WE MEET TOO LATE

We meet too late,
Too bound by other ties
Of heart and mind,
To let ourselves be tangled
In this tightening web,
Woven from the shy and tender strands
Which, spider-like,
The heart puts forth
To bridge the emptiness.

We meet too late,
Too laden with impedimenta of the past,
Too smugly sewn
Into the closely-fitting shroud
Of habitude,
To dare the fearful rending
Which would leave us naked
To the world.

We meet too late
For love,
So let us play
At being friends,
And try to hide the sadness
That we feel.

GERONTIKOS

Where now
That flowering plain
Where once a star-wracked youth
Reached in his virgin mind
Toward things unseen
Beyond the curving knife-edge
Of his world?
Where now
That radiant dome of sky
Toward which he soared,
Daring with pride of innocence
The long swift fall from grace?

The Earth, alas, grows old beneath our aging feet;
And here,
Where once was flowering plain,
An old man squats amid the bleeding thorns,
Waiting in silent terror
The cruel rebirth of innocence;
While high above,
Where once was radiant sky,
A vulture wheels.

STRANGE LAND

Ask not that I forget you,
For you have led me through
A strange land:

A land dark —
But lit betimes with blinding light;

A land flat —
But marked betimes with soaring heights;

A land silent —
But loud betimes with angel's songs.

A land lonely —
But . . .
Yes, a land lonely.

Ask not that I forget you.

IF LOVE BE THESE

This you have taught me:
That love
Is not a soft and yielding thing
But hard as diamonds,
Remote and cold
As an alpine peak.

And this I would teach to you:
That deep beneath that austere peak
Lies a core of fire,
That incandescent womb
In which the cutting edge of love
Is tempered
Before it thrusts itself
Toward heaven.

But if love be these:
The frost of stone,
The scorch of flame,
Then let us ask not of it
That it comfort us.

TO RICARDO

I found you
Squatting naked
At the crumbling edges of the world,
Sifting the dry gray rubble of your mind
In search of some almost-remembered
Clue.

I found you
Crouching there
On the rim of doom
In sleepless silence,
Straining the heart's attentive ear
To catch one sound, one word,
One note of music,
That would say to you "Turn back".

I found you there
But, weeping, turned away,
That I not be the one
To tell you
No clue would come,
No sound be heard
Except the rustle of dark wings
Above the void's cruel brink.

THREE POEMS IN HAIKU FORM

Urn of Memory,
What do you contain but the
Ashes of desire?

* *
*

The cobra dreams of
Love and feels her cold blood warmed
By distant lightning.

* *
*

Is it not enough
That the Universe exists?
Need we invent God?

DEMETRIA IN THE
SCULPTURE GARDEN

This brooding twilight,
Balanced on the verge of night
And rain,
Lies like a shroud
Upon the chill damp ponderous
Bronze
Of graven breast and thigh—
Dead fruit of passion's living hand,
Frozen beauty
Trapped in the *rigor mortis*
Of its last mute ecstasy.

I pause among these sombre icons
To cup a cold unyielding breast;
And suddenly
My mind flees from this place
In search of warmth,
Of sun and flesh,
Of breath and glance.

I turn to go
And at my elbow,
As though conjured by the thought,
You stand
Waiting,
Your patina the sun-gold of a Cretan summer,
Your smile the flickering play of light and shadow
Of an Attic afternoon,

The first shy drop of evening rain
Glistening like a tear
Upon your cheek.

I reach out
To touch your warmth
But you are gone,
Leaving me with empty hand
Outstretched,
Another lifeless figure
In this garden of the dead.

WE WHO WEAR OUR DRUNKENNESS
WITH DIGNITY

We who don each night
The guardian veil
Of insobriety,
That we may not be known
Too well,
That we may dare to speak aloud
Of common things
And not betray
The anguished secrets of our hearts—
We who don each night
The guardian veil
Can say at least
That we do wear our drunkenness
With dignity.

I DO NOT FEAR TO WALK
AMONG MY FATHERS' BONES

I do not fear
To walk among my fathers' bones,
Sown through the dim ancestral cloisters
Of the mind;
Nor do I fear,
In the long New England night,
To dare their ghosts,
Chanting their litany of doom
Against the keening
Of the northern winds.

My dread is other:
Of crossing over to their side
And spending all of death's eternities
Among their kind,
Rising from rotting tombs
To ride the wind
And vent the bitterness
Of shipwrecked dreams,
Fog-bound horizons of the soul,
And, most terrible of all,
Envy of those who live
And love.

ARCANUM

Doubt not that it exists,
Somewhere at the quiet center
Of this mortal storm,
That hidden place from which,
New-born,
We groped our way
Unseeing
Out through the womb-like darkness
Into the turmoiled world.

Doubt not that it exists,
But seek not to return;
For we have come too far,
Not knowing even
Why and how we came,
Recalling nothing of that secret place
Except perhaps
A phantom memory
Of primal innocence
Forsaken there.

TRISTAN'S LAY, OFF CORNWALL

It is done,
Yseulte;
We have drunk together
From Brangäne's cup.

The mind, perhaps,
Was ill-prepared;
But not the heart,
Whose ancient wisdom
Long foresaw
This confluence of destinies,
This sealing of a fated pact,
Which binds us now till death.

But death will come too soon,
Yseulte,
So let us ride the sea's dark shoreward surge
In one last fierce embrace,
One night-long song of love
Whose echo neither dawn nor Cornwall's coast
Nor Cornwall's King nor all of time
Will still.

PRAYER FOR CHRISTMAS

Forgive us, God, our knowledge.
Forgive our having glimpsed,
In one dark flash
Of unforgotten terror,
Thy face.

Forgive us, God,
If, having seen,
We flee Thy sight,
That we be saved
Not by, but from
Thy will.

Forgive us, God, our prayer
That Thou may be reborn this night
In innocence,
That we, Thy frightened children,
May once again believe in Thee.

MARÉE

The warm, unhurried tide,
Flowing black as blood
Through buried veins,
Bears me to you
On some unseen
And unimagined shore.

Toward what new life
Or death
This current runs
I dare not ask.
But you will wait
And I shall find you there
And we will know.

WHEN ONE HAS MADE A LIFE
OF WAITING

When one has made a life
Of waiting,
One waits easily,
With a certain grace
Belying the deepening desperation
Of the heart.

When one has made a life
Of waiting,
One faces the vacant stare
Of dead horizons
Calmly,
Turning away
With each returning empty dawn
To think on other things.

When one has made a life
Of waiting,
One dares no longer hope;
Nor dares abandon hope,
Knowing that time
And the gnawing hunger of the heart
Have made a home for love,
If only it will come.

NIGHT WAVE

Must this, then, be your unproud end,
Summoning your last remaining strength
To crest and break,
Unseen, unheard, except by me,
Upon this night-enshrouded beach?

Where now the golden dawn
In which the restless deep
From out her fathomed loins
Did give you forth
And launch you landward,
Lusty in your gathering might,
To hurl your awesome sinewed weight
In blaze of noon
Against the trembling ramparts
Of some hostile shore?

Where now the glory?
Not here upon this dark and unfrequented strand;
Not here or anywhere
For now the chance is lost,
The orgasmic moment past,
Your very imprint washed away
Before the echo of your passing dies.

The rasping threnody of gulls
Drifts down the wind
And you are gone —
With none but me to know
That you were here.

TO THE KING'S DARK DAUGHTER

You called
And I,
Waking from a sleep that was no sleep
But more the heart's paralysis,
Reached out to you
And touched but shadows,
For you,
Fearing the heart's mute hunger,
Had slipped away.

But the hungry heart,
Once wakened,
Rests not easily again,
Following the spoor of its desire,
Pursuing the music of its dream,
Until its quarry tires
And runs no more,
Turning at last to face its choice.

As you one day will turn,
Dark princess,
To embrace your hunter
Or to slay him with the quick bright sword
Of your contempt.

FINAL AUTUMN

There was a time
When Autumn came in Spring,
When youth's exuberance
Was shield against the poignancy
Of Nature's slow withdrawal
Into death.

There was a time
When Autumn fell in Summer,
In the bold meridian of our days,
When falling leaves
Bore no more portent
Than the lengthening shadows
Of an August afternoon.

But now the time is here
When Autumn comes,
Not as an unmarked episode
In Spring,
Not as the careless afternoon
Of yet another Summer's day,
But as the penultimate season
Of our lives;
The last but one,
Which is the Winter
In whose frozen fastness
The eternal round of seasons
For us will end.

POUR LA FEMME INCONNUE

I have entered into you
And found darkness
Waiting —
Like a pitfall
In the jungle night.

I have entered into you
And found silence
Waiting —
Like the soundless void
Of distant space.

I have entered into you,
Blind with darkness,
Deaf with silence,
And have found you not;
But only felt you there
Crouching like a great cat
Across the dark and still
Abyss.

THE WATCHERS

I have watched them
Watching me,
Thinking themselves unseen;
I have traced their cruel ophidian stare
Back to the shadows
Where they nest
And have even heard them,
When the wind is right,
Clucking to one another
In an unknown tongue.

I have seen them, heard them,
And yet I know not who
Or what they are,
Or what it is they want of me.

I do not know,
And do not dare to ask.

VOYAGE 109, OUTBOUND

Dawn,
And the waking eye,
Lifting the veil of sleep,
Gropes through the morning mists
Toward shore,
Straining to raise
The slumbering Pernambuco coast,
Stretched like a sleeping beast
Across the sea's glass top.

Dawn,
And the eye of memory
Turns back
To roam the tender landscape
Of the flesh,
To trace again
The well-remembered contours
Of that fragrant land,
To clasp the hills
And course the flowing valleys
Down to that wooded shrine
Whose mystery
Renews itself in recollect.

Dawn,
And the heart turns painfully away
From love recalled,
To face the vacant day.

SOUTHAMPTON BEACH

Rebirth?
Then I would have it happen here,
Thrust from the sea's deep womb
To lie on these harrowed dunes
Like the bone-gray driftwood,
New-come but aged in the brine
Of years (and tears),
With heart like weathered oak,
Impervious to hurt.

But then —
Impervious to hurt
Must mean
Impervious to joy,
To ecstasy.

So should I best remain,
This second time,
Unborn.

IN REMEMBRANCE OF A FRIEND

He drained life quickly,
In avid gulps
As from a leaking cup,
Afraid that something might escape
Before he got it down.

He drained life greedily,
Grimacing from time to time
At unexpected bitterness,
But mostly relishing
The rich dark brew.

He drained life eagerly
Until,
Reaching the sodden dregs,
He paused and laughed
And threw the cup away.

FOR ELANA

I have seen your white hands,
In the night's hiatus,
Drifting like gulls
Across the mind's dim dream-washed shores.

I have seen your white hands,
In the night's hiatus,
Floating like doves
Above the deep abysses of the heart.

I have seen your white hands,
In the night's hiatus,
Hovering like egrets
Over the dark Priapic wood.

I have reached out
For your white hands,
In the night's hiatus,
And touched but moonbeams.

DIALOGUE NO. 2

Do you believe in God?

> I would reverse the question:
> Does God believe in me?

Then you do believe that God exists?

> Not necessarily.

But if He does not exist,
Then how can He believe in you?

> If I knew that He did not exist,
> The answer would be obvious.

Then you do accept the possibility
Of His existence?

> I accept as theoretically possible
> The existence of many things
> In which I do not believe.

But why did you pose the question
A moment ago
Of whether God believes in you?

> Because that is the crucial question
> And one whose answer,
> Could one but give it,
> Would prove if God exists or not.

How so?

It is very simple:
If God existed
He would believe in me;
If He does not believe in me
Then He does not exist.

But you, it would seem,
Do not believe in Him;
Yet you exist.

Of course.
For Man can still exist
Without belief in God;
But God cannot exist
Without belief in Man.

And does this point of view
Help you to know
If God exists or not?

Not at all,
For this is something one can never know.
But at least it shifts the onus
Of unbelief
From me to God,
So that I can stop worrying
(As you are always worrying)
And get on about my work.

I SLEEP NEAR DEATH

I sleep near Death,
In that long cold shadow
Which falls along the dark north coast
Where white whales
Dance their ponderous pavane
Mid wasting monoliths
Of dying ice.

I sleep near Death,
On virgin sheets of fallen snow
Beneath the skull-dome
Of the night,
While one by one
The stars
Drop from their blackened sockets
Like ripened fruit.

I sleep near Death,
And dream, dream, dream
Of Life.

WAKE NOT YET, MY LOVE

Wake not yet, my love.
This is the precious hour
Of innocence,
The cool of dawn
When Nature,
Drained of all passion
By the night,
Becomes a child once more.

This is the solitary moment of surcease,
Here in the sheltered grove of morn
Between the haunted forest of the night
And sun-beat, skull-strewn desert of the day.

Here and here alone is peace;
While you beside me,
Locked in the womb of sleep,
Wait to be born again.

THOUGHTS ON A NOVEMBER SUNSET
IN NORTHERN MICHIGAN

Time, after all, runs on,
And now the age is past
When Hokusai,
Turning westward with the bend
Of famed Tokkaido's shore-borne course,
Did pause and gaze and wet his brush
To fasten in his aging mind
The garish colors of a sunset
Hung like fire
Behind the Kamakura hills —
      Art imitating Nature
      For posterity.

His age is past,
Yet now,
A century and half a world away,
This flaming scroll
Unfurls across the west,
Turning these Nordic lakes
To pools of icy fire
Among the prostrate winter-stricken hills:
Old Hokusai's sunset come to life once more —
      A fleeting tribute
      Which Nature now repays to Art.

WHY MUST THE NIGHT BE HAUNTED SO?

Why must the night
Be haunted so?
Why must the hours of darkness
Be the hours of truth?
Why must the past return
Each night
To unhinge the doors of memory,
Opening up forbidden rooms,
Awakening ghosts best left asleep?

Why must the night
Be haunted so,
When all that sanity demands
Is the anaesthesia of sleep?

ODE (IN HAIKU FORM)
TO THE YOUNG FRENCH WAITRESS IN
THE CLUB DINING ROOM

Like a dew-damp rose
You bring the memory of
Spring to aging men:

The sight of beauty,
To refresh their dimming view
Of grace remembered;

The scent of flowers,
To waken in their dead souls
Dreams of youth and love;

The echo of songs
Too long silent, whose music
Stirs their tired loins.

I too feel your spell
And, if I dared, would thrust these
Lines into your hand:

Comme la rose, amour,
Tu me plais, et comme la rose
Ouvres-toi à moi.

THE AUTUMN-BORN

Where does one go,
Born in Autumn;
Which is the way one takes
To Death?

The short sure way,
Taken step by grudging step;
The tottering gray road
To the Winter of oblivion?

That was the way my Father took.

Or the hurrying, dangerous, winding way
Against the sweep of seasons,
Back to — what?

That was the way *his* Father chose.

And I —
Caught in the line of Autumn-born,
Prisoner of the alternating pattern of the blood —
Must be the heir of him who, once-removed,
Did choose the uncertain way;
Doomed, like him,
To struggle back from Autumn
Through an aging Summer
To die amid the snows of Spring.

But how to tell my son?

BATTLEFIELD

I lie across you
Like a warrior dead
Across his fallen foe.
For we have slain each other,
Here, this night,
Upon this perfumed battleground
Of rutted linen.

We have traded mortal wound
For mortal wound:
I, with this cruel and mindless blade,
Have torn apart
The satin texture
Of your heart's virginity;
While you,
In desperate riposte,
Have rent my soul's last refuge
From itself.

And so we lie,
Knowing we are dead
But knowing too
That we must rise again,
At long night's end,
To go about our lives
As though this duel to death
Had been but one more
Minuet.

MAY NOT AN OLD MAN DREAM?

May not an old man dream?

Has not an old man
Earned the right
To shed for once
The ashen garments of an empty Now,
To don again the iridescent plumage
Of a time in Spring
When Love and Beauty
Bore him on untiring wings
Across the flowering Earth?

May not an old man dream?

Then wake me not
To sup the evening gruel,
But let me dine this one last time
On festive fare of passion's dream
Relived:
Tasting the dew of hidden roses,
Drinking the nectar from breasts
Heavy with love,
Devouring the fragrant flesh
Of youth.

So let me dream,
And wake me but in time to die.

TO WHERE I WAIT

I have clamped the shackles
Of my will
Upon these hands,
Which nothing crave so much
As to reach out and touch your cheek.

I have locked the fetters
Of decorum
Upon these feet,
Which want naught
But to run
To where you are.

I have even curbed this brain,
Which would seek each moment
To conjure up the icon
Of your face.

I have bound these hands,
These feet,
This brain —
But not this errant heart,
Which runs free down the winds
Of its desire
To follow you through day and night
In all your moods and tempers
And in the arching grace
Of every motion,
Until that time when you at last will pause,

Turn back,
Then find your way cross half a world,
Or but across a room,
To where I wait.

I FEAR THE POEMS I WRITE

I fear the poems I write.
I dread the awful message
Which they bring,
Encrypted in the deep inferno
Of the soul
To be deciphered
At the edge of madness
Into the counterfeit of words
Whose hidden terror
Only I can read.

I fear the poems I write.
But even more I fear
Those dark unwritten thoughts,
Hanging like sleeping bats
In dank malignant caves,
Waiting to be wakened in some golgothan night
To sweep away all words, all poems, all sanity.

THE SOUND BENEATH THE SOUND

I hear it now,
When the night wind dies
And the birdsongs end;
I hear it now,
The sound beneath the sound,
The gentle rustling
In the dovecotes of the memory,
The haunting strains
Which etch upon the heart
The sad soft music of regret.

I hear it now
And, hearing,
Turn
And draw the stillness of the night
About my ears,
That I may sleep.

WINTER PARTING

Soon it will come —
The unsweet sorrow of our parting,
The fumbling motions of farewell,
The unuttered words
Sealed deep within
Behind that rusting lock for which
Once more
No key appears.

Soon it will come —
The dreaded moment of your going,
To find me wordless,
Unspeaking in the taut and grieving way
Of children
Faced with the bafflement of loss.

Soon it will come —
And there will be no you,
But only emptiness of winter's night
And sound of owls along the dark road
Back to loneliness.

SEOUL: SPRING 1953

Spring comes not gladly back this year,
To face anew the witless stare
Of vacant ruins,
Waiting like threadbare children
To be garlanded
In lilac blooms.

Spring comes not gladly back,
To hear her early thunder
Merge once more with sound of guns
Borne southward on the winds of war.

Spring comes not gladly back,
To see again
The lethal chalk-lines
Traced by unseen birds of prey
Across the blue slate
Of the wind-swept sky.

Spring comes not gladly back,
To find new wounds, new scars, new graves
Slashed in the raw and aching flesh
Of this untranquil Land of Morning Calm

Spring comes not gladly back this year,
But sadly, shyly comes,
Bringing the balm of hope's rebirth:
That from these vernal buds
May this time bloom the flower
Of Peace.

NIGHTSONG

Here,
In the still eye
Of this storm of ghosts
Which is the night,
I find you waiting
To take me home to you:
Home to the crystal pathways of the mind,
Home to the sunlit highlands of the spirit,
Home to the secret places of the flesh.

For each of us
Is progenitor and progeny and lover
To the other,
Each having given birth
To each,
Both finding in the other
That missing part
Without which one must live
The crippled life of loneliness.

Here,
In the still eye
Of this storm of ghosts
Which is the night,
I dream your coming,
Then wake to find you gone.

PRAYER AT SEA

If You will not meet me here,
God,
In the sea's dark wasteland,
Then where?

If You will not keep this rendezvous,
Here where the moon-sucked tides
Burgeon like driven clouds
Across a drowned Atlantis' stormy skies,
Then why?

If You will not dare this night,
God,
Then do not ever come,
For You will find me gone.

I HAVE MET WITH FACELESS MEN

I have met with
Faceless men
On nameless streets
In unremembered cities
Across the Earth,
Consummating furtive deals
By night,
My currency the lives of strangers
Who did never do me ill.

For better or for worse
The work is done,
And I am dying
From the memory.

TO GIOVANNA

Will you understand
How I, grown old,
Remember you so well?
Will you recall
What once you must have known
(With heart if not with mind),
That I did love you —
Not as the girl whom others saw
But as a woman,
Bearing within herself
The sadness and the beauty
Of a timeless past?

Will you remember,
Or will you turn to someone at your side
And ask:
"Who is that aging gentleman
Across the room
Who seems to think he knows me
Yet dares not speak?"

QUINQUAGENARY ELEGY

I sit here
On a borrowed terrace
In the whey-thin sunlight
Of my half-a-hundredth year
And think of Death,
Feeling it stir in the womb of Time,
Feeling it grow
From that seed implanted fifty winters past,
Feeling it test its strength
And start to count the impatient days.

Somewhere
In the shadowed chambers
Of the memory
Must lie some arcane clue,
Some undeciphered message,
Which would tell me why,
For love of God,
It must be thus.

But I seek in vain,
Find not,
So go on sitting
On a borrowed terrace
To await, uncomprehending,
The ripening of the seed.

I HAVE HEARD THE GODS

I have heard the thundering converse
Of the Gods
Across the echoing peaks,
And listened to them
Whispering
Beneath the night.
I have heard their roistering songs
At dawn
Where distant oceans
Stretch to the edges of the world;
Have felt the pause when,
Tired of speaking,
They join their silence
To the hush of eventide.

I have heard the Gods
In all their changing moods;
But still I listen for that smaller voice,
That nearer voice,
Whose words alone can touch my heart.

THERE IS A TIME

There is a time
In yearning's long and weary pilgrimage
When the heart must rest,
When the mind must sleep,
When the anodyne of hope
Must be withdrawn.

There is a time
In the lonely hungering quest for love
When the search must end,
When the youthful vow of fealty
Must be renounced,
When the great illusion,
Sustained alone by hope,
Must forever be dispelled.

There is a time
(Can it be now?)
When hope's extinction is the sacrifice
Which life must make
If it is to endure.

THE CITADEL

Build high and strong
If you would wall out Love.
If this must be your citadel
Then leave no gaps in its encircling wall,
No gate through which,
In innocent disguise,
That gentle Sorcerer
Might enter in,
No window-slits through which to gaze upon
The unwalled beauty there beyond
And make you doubt.

Add, too, a massive dome of stone
Lest even sight of heaven's blue,
Embroidered with the arching flight of birds,
Might undermine your cause.
Shut out the stars and moon
Whose silent beauty,
Through the long and lonely watches of the night,
Would but corrode
The chaste and brittle armor of your will.

And when your citadel is built,
Impregnable against the proffered gift
Of Love,
Try then to think not
Of the one who waits without.

A WORD TO POETS

I would say this to you Poets:
That once I called myself Poet
(As other men have called themselves God),
Until that day when first I understood
That poetry's golden thread
Can only come
From the unraveling of the soul;
That as the thread grows
The fabric of the soul diminishes,
So that the Poet must find himself one day
Soulless,
With only skeins of golden thread
To prove that once he had a soul.

This I discovered,
And stopped in time.
So now I sit and count my tarnished skeins
And meditate upon
The tattered fabric that remains,
Giving thanks that this at least
Was saved.

Yes, I stopped in time.
But you?

I GO DOWN ANGRY

I go down angry
Upon the vast unfeatured plains,
Looking back in bitter sorrow
To dreams of excellence
Abandoned
On the cold high peaks
Above.

I go down angry,
Unspeaking,
To find myself
Accepted member of the brotherhood
Of men
Who rule the plains
And do not ask
Who rules the peaks.

THINK NOT ILL OF ME

Think not ill of me
If I reach out,
Unspeaking,
To touch your cheek
Or take your hand in mine.

Think not ill of me,
Nor draw away,
But wait
And let the moment pass
Quietly,
Till I can summon up
The cowardice
To turn away from love.

I AM FROM A SOLEMN TRIBE
DESCENDED

I am
From a solemn tribe
Descended,
A race which,
Lashed by fear
Of God's high vengeance,
Has scaled the scarp of history
Unsmiling,
Dragging its weight of conscience
Upward
Toward the nurtured myth
Of final absolution.

I am
From this solemn tribe
Descended,
Prisoner of the blood,
Condemned
To bear my heritage of guilt
Up the Sisyphean slope,
While knowing
That no absolution waits.

POETRY OF SILENCE

I

Lead me back, God,
To that stillness
Out of which I came.
Teach me once more to speak
Without words.
Teach me once more, God,
The poetry of silence.

II

TESTAMENT

I

I would die in the sun's fierce flame,
A sudden incandescent pyre,
Reduced to swirling ash
With the final agonizing breath.

I would meet death locked in the cold embrace
Of glacial ice,
Buried deep in its prehistoric womb,
Borne slowly seaward
Down the slopes of centuries
Toward oblivion.

I would give up life in the verdant depths
Of some far hidden jungle
Known but to roaming carnivores,
That they alone perform the funeral rite,
Leaving no remnants
But the bones they carry off to secret caves
To gnaw in peace.

I would die thus,
Bearing away beyond all reach
The outworn chrysalis of life,
That none might violate the awful privacy
Of death.

II

I would die thus;
But lest death's triumph be complete
I would leave behind
Some little thing,
Some relic crafted by my hand alone,
Some hieroglyphic graven on a hidden wall
To be found, deciphered,
And one day understood.

I would leave behind
One moment out of time
Which I alone have filled with meaning,
One moment caught and held, transfixed
In the clear dark amber of eternal memory.

I would leave behind
Some part of me,
Indestructible by fire or flood or wars
     or surge of time,
To mark this harried passage
Through mortality.

III

I would die thus;
But I would leave behind
A poem,
Wrought from the deep despair
And joyous ecstasy
Of life:

    A poem — this relic crafted by my hand alone;
    A poem — this hieroglyphic graven on a hidden wall;
    A poem — this pregnant moment out of time;
    A poem — this small enduring part of me.

Thus would I die,
And thus would I live
Beyond the dying.

About the Author

In the Old World tradition of the Poet-Diplomat, Niles Bond began to write poetry early in his thirty-year diplomatic career. Although many of the poems in this book were written far from his native shores, while serving in such areas of the world as Western Europe, Northeast Asia, and South America, they reveal few geographical coordinates. His poetic terrain is rather the inner landscape of the human condition, which he explores in an intensely personal way.

Mr. Bond was born and raised in and around Boston and now lives with his wife, also a writer, in Old Lyme, Connecticut. His two previous books of poetry were published to critical acclaim in Brazil in 1965 and 1967.

This book was produced for the publisher by
Ray Freiman & Company
Stamford, Connecticut 06903